ROCK
RIFFS
FOR GUITAR

by John Stix and Yoichi Arakawa

ISBN 0-7935-4372-X

POCKET GUIDE

HAL•LEONARD®
CORPORATION

7777 W. BLUEMOUND RD. P.O. BOX 13819 MILWAUKEE, WI 53213

CONTENTS

INTRODUCTION

Mariah Carey and Black Sabbath are both looking to do the same thing with their music. Each of them hope to present songs that stay with you for the long haul. They are both trying to hook you. In pop music, the hook is found in the melody. In all forms of rock, be it metal, alternative, hard rock, blues rock, the hook is found in the riff. Where Boyz II Men ask you to sing along, Led Zeppelin invite you to pick up the air guitar. How many people know all the words to Deep Purple's "Smoke on the Water?" How many more people know the riff "Dun dun dun, dun dun dun-dun, dun dun dun, dun-dun?" Cool riffs and classic melodies are not mutually exclusive. The greatest bands, like The Beatles, have it both ways, with songs like "Day Tripper" and "Birthday."

Rock Riffs For Guitar is designed to show you how some of the finest guitarists used simple lines to create memorable song hooks. Mostly, the authors hope this book will be inspirational in getting you to write your own timeless riffs, perhaps by altering some of the lines you learn here. To get the pro's opinion, we went to guitarists from Pantera's Diamond Darrell to Collective Soul's Ed Roland, and asked them for the riffs that changed their life.

We've presented here 114 riffs divided into five sections: Single-Note Riffs, Combining Single-Notes With Chords, Power-Chord Riffs, Chord-Strumming Riffs, and Arpeggio Riffs. Just spend as much time as you need with the tablature explanation, and then riff out to your heart's content.

EXPLAINING TABLATURE

Tablature is a paint-by-number language telling you which notes to play on the fingerboard. Each of the six lines represents a string on the guitar. The numbers in the line indicate which frets to press down. Note that tablature does not indicate the rhythm.

1st string	E
2nd string	B
3rd string	G
4th string	D
5th string	A
6th string	E

NOTATION LEGEND

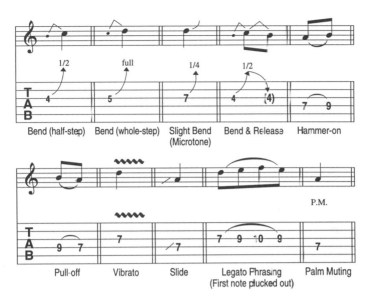

Bend (whole step):
Pick the note and bend up a whole step (two frets).

Slight Bend (microtone):
Pick the note and bend up slightly. A microtone is less than a half step (one fret).

Bend & Release:
Pick the note and bend up a whole step, then release the bend back to the original note. All three notes are tied together; only the first note is attacked.

Hammer-on:
Pick the first (lower) note, then "hammer-on" to sound the higher note with another finger by fretting it without picking.

Pull-off:
Place both fingers on the notes to be sounded. Pick the first (higher) note, then sound the lower note by "pulling-off" the finger on the higher note while keeping the lower note fretted.

Slide:
Strike the first note, and then, without striking it again, use the same left-hand finger to slide up or down the string to the second note.

Legato Phrasing:
A series of notes where only the first note is picked and the rest are played with hammer-ons and pull-offs.

Palm Muting:
A note or notes are played with the picking hand resting on the strings, muting the ring of each note, and adding a percussive sound in its place.

Usually a good song is a very simple thing, and you've got to open yourself up to that. Sometimes the simplest things are the coolest. I always think in terms of a hook, something to latch onto. You try and use that as a building block. I usually start with a riff, or a hook, or a chord change, and mold it so it goes somewhere.

Sometimes I'll sit down with Steven (Tyler) and we'll draw on a certain song. I'll say, "Wouldn't it be neat to write a song like something that really knocked us out when we were 15?" We went to see Keith Richards, and he played "Connection" in the show. We were thinking about how cool that song was and how cool The Kinks and that kind of English pop-rock was. I started playing a riff like that, and Steven's at the keyboard. By the end of the afternoon we had "My Girl." I think it's a tip of the hat to those songs from the '60s.

You discover riffs all different ways. If you do anything one way, it gets stale very fast. The riff to "Walk This Way" was written at a soundcheck in Hawaii. Sometimes I won't touch a guitar for days, and when I pick it up is when I get some of the best things. That's because you're not into your scales or whatever you've been practicing. The riff to "F.I.N.E." came out in as long as it took to play it. Sometimes you can have a terrible day and that's what does it. Sometimes you've got to have an attitude. But you can't actually be angry. I used to think that's what it was. It would be really good to let the dog bite you and you'd come out with some good stuff. Anger is good, but you end up realizing you play good in spite of anger. It's more like attitude and getting out some aggression. Speed metal doesn't do anything for me. I like the real power rock stuff like Deep Purple and Metallica. I still get goose bumps when I hear "Immigrant Song." "Love in an Elevator" was an interesting riff that needed a song around it. For "Don't Get Mad Get Even" I put on "Rag Doll" backwards and tried to play along with it. I got a chord change and built it from there.

—*Joe Perry (Aerosmith)**

**Courtesy of *Guitar for the Practicing Musician Magazine*

SINGLE-NOTE RIFFS

You will probably recognize many of the following riffs. They are all made up of single-note lines. The Blues Scale and the Minor Pentatonic Scale are the most common sources for rock and blues guitar riffs and solos. Artists from Nirvana to Pink Floyd dip into the same pool of notes to write their riffs.

For a short review of these scales, refer to the *Pocket Guides to Major and Minor Pentatonic Scales,* and *Basic Blues.*

Ex. 1 is reminiscent of Led Zeppelin's "Heartbreaker." Notice that the riff opens with the first five notes of the A Blues Scale (A,C, D, D#, E, G), played in order. In the hands of a composer like Jimmy Page, even a consecutive scale pattern can become a classic.

Ex. 1

Ex. 2 was inspired by Jack Bruce's line from Cream's "Sunshine of Your Love." Notice that they have used all the notes of the D Blues Scale (D,F,G,Ab,A,C). Cream bassist Jack Bruce said the riff was composed on an upright bass one early dawn.

Ex. 2

Ex. 3 is an Aeromsith-like line from "Walk This Way." The notes are from the E Blues Scale (E,G,A,Bb,B,D).

Ex. 3

Ex. 4 is similar to the "Aqualung" riff from Jethro Tull. Just like "Heartbreaker," this riff uses the first five notes of the six-note blues scale, here played in G (G,B♭,C,D♭,D,F).

Ex. 4

Ex. 5 is a Nirvana-like line inspired by "Come As You Are." It too uses five out of six notes in the blues scale, this time leaving out the D of the B Blues Scale (B,D,E,F,F♯,A).

Ex. 5

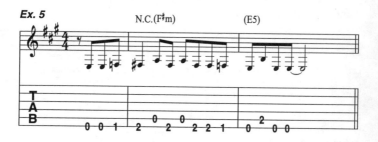

Ex. 6 reminds us of a line from "I Want to Take You Higher" by Sly and the Family Stone. This descending line uses the notes of the B Blues Scale (B,D,E,F,F♯,A).

Ex. 6

Ex. 7 is another descending riff, similar to Ex. 6. But this one resembles Rick Derringer's "Rock 'n' Roll Hootchie Koo."

Ex. 7

I turned the rhythm from "Willie and the Hand Jive" into the verse.
—Rick Derringer on "Rock and Roll Hoochie Koo"

8

Ex. 8 is similar to a line Leslie West played in Mountain's "Never In My Life." The Blues Scale used this time is G♯, (G♯,B,C♯,D, D♯,F♯).

Ex. 9 is the first in our section of single-note riffs based on the pentatonic (five-note) scale. This riff was inspired by a line from Pink Floyd's "Money." This riff uses the notes of the D Major Pentatonic (D,E,F♯,A,B,).

Ex. 10 is similar to "Purple Haze" by Jimi Hendrix.

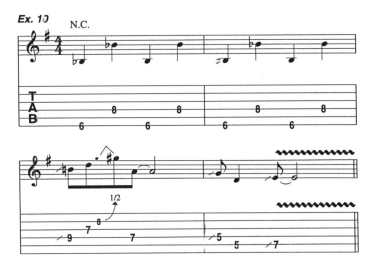

Ex. 11 is another Hendrix-inspired riff. This one is a reflection of Jimi Hendrix's "I Don't' Live Today" using B Minor Pentatonic Scale (B,D,E,F♯,A).

Ex. 12 is a funky little pentatonic riff inspired by Les McCann's piano line from "Compared to What." Though this riff is made up of only a few notes, notice how the syncopated rhythm creates a good groove. Remember that rhythm is just as important as note choice when it comes to composing a classic riff.

Ex. 13 is in the vein of Led Zeppelin's "Moby Dick." This riff is played with a dropped D tuning, which means the low E string is tuned a whole step down to D.

Ex. 14 is a reflection of a classic Albert King G Minor Pentatonic riff (G,B♭,C,D,F) from "Born Under a Bad Sign."

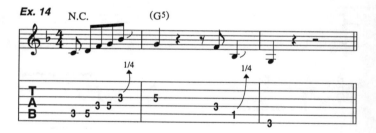

Ex. 15 is a take on Lenny Kravitz's "Are You Gonna Go My Way." This riff comes from E Minor Pentatonic Scale (E,G,A,B,D).

Ex. 16 is similar to a riff from "Life in the Fast Lane," by
The Eagles.

*"I'm A Man" by The Yardbirds is as classic as the original
(Muddy Waters). It's what they did with a simple riff to make it
more of a song. It's another case of taking it to the limits. It's just
a cool guitar move that builds up with the bass.*
                                                    —Joe Perry (Aerosmith)

*Three riffs that changed my life were "Over the Edge" by The
Wipers, "Stone Cold Fever" from Humble Pie, but that was only
for when I was a drummer. "Not Right" by The Stooges, and
"Can't You Hear Me Knocking" by The Rolling Stones. After Mick
Taylor left, The Stones lost it.*
                                                    —J Mascis (Dinosaur Jr.)

Obviously, not all single-note riffs are based on Pentatonic
or Blues scales. The following riffs were based on other
scales.

Ex. 17 was inspired by the opening riff of Metallica's "Enter
Sandman."

Ex. 18 is similar to a riff from Offspring's "Come Out and
Play."

Ex. 19 is reminiscent of the G Major Scale (G,A,B,C,D,E,F♯)-based riff from "Billy Jean," by Michael Jackson.

Ex. 20 is similar to the classic riff from Heart's "Crazy on You." This riff comes from the A Natural Minor Scale (A,B,C,D,E,F,G).

Ex. 21 is a take on a Jimi Hendrix groove riff from "Manic Depression," in 3/4.

Ex. 22 is similar to a riff from "Misty Mountain Hop" by Led Zeppelin. Notice how the syncopated rhythm with open strings creates a groove.

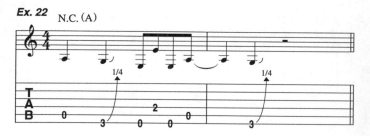

Ex. 23 has its roots in Led Zeppelin's "Immigrant Song." The riff uses only two notes an octave apart!

Ex. 24 reminds us of Metallica's "Jump In The Fire."

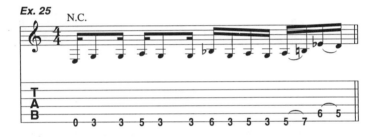

Ex. 25 is a take on a Pantera's riff from "Cowboys From Hell."

Ex. 26 was inspired by an Anthrax riff from "Caught in the Mosh." Note the power of riff is created by the open string and the gradually ascending notes.

Ex. 27 is our reflection of the riff to Ozzy Osbourne's "Crazy Train." The riff consists entirely of 8th notes based on the F# Aeolian Mode (F#,G#,A,B,C#,D,E) Notice the first bar uses an F# pedal-tone, building tension.

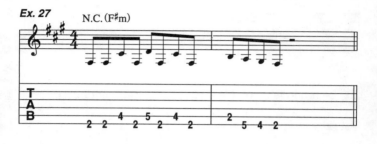

Ex. 28 is similar to a Jimi Hendrix riff from "Burning of the Midnight Lamp." The riff draws life from the C Major Scale (C,D,E,F,G,A,B,). Again notice that the riff consists of only 8th notes.

Ex. 29 is a tough little riff inspired by Jeff Beck's version of "I Ain't Superstitious."

Ex. 30 is a take on David Bowie's "The Man Who Sold the World."

Ex. 31 relies on simplicity and its repetition throughout the song, to leave its mark. This is reminiscent of The Rolling Stones' "Satisfaction."

Ex. 31

Ex. 32 has roots in the Led Zeppelin riff from "Dazed and Confused." Half-step bending is the key to making this riff speak.

Ex. 32

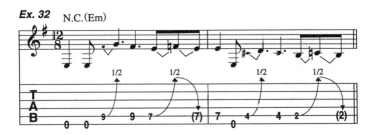

Ex. 33 was inspired by The Beatles song "I Feel Fine." Notice how the notes in the first bar outline the D7sus4 chord.

Ex. 33

Ex. 34 is a reflection of the Led Zeppelin riff from "The Ocean." Notice the time signature changes in the second bar.

Ex. 34

Ex. 35 is a take on Soundgarden's "Superunknown." This riff uses legato phrasing.

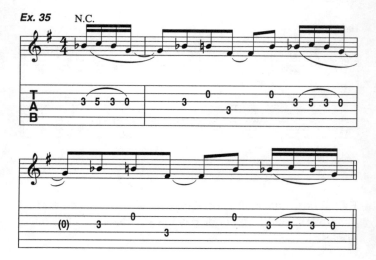

Ex. 36 is a riff arranged from a bass line that originally involves a little slapping, a little popping, and an open string bass pedal. The riff is based on The Red Hot Chili Peppers' cover of Stevie Wonders' "Higher Ground."

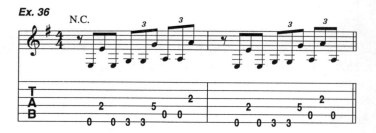

The first lick I can remember trying to play as a kid was "Life in the Fast Lane." I was so happy I could get it. It took me so long to get it.

—Ed Roland (Collective Soul)

The three riffs that changed my life are Ozzy Osbourne's "Crazy Train," "Eruption" by Van Halen, and "She" by Kiss. "Smoke on the Water" was the first one I ever did. The one out of those would definitely have to be "Crazy Train." When that first came out, the sound of that guitar and that riff was amazing.

—Diamond Darrell (Pantera)

RIFFS COMBINING SINGLE NOTES WITH CHORDS

This section shows you the extension of the single-note riff, where it combines with two- or three-note chords.

Ex. 37 is in the style of Van Halen's version of The Kinks' song, "You Really Got Me."

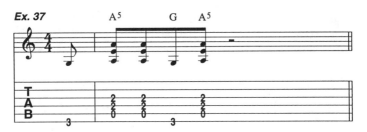

Ex. 38 takes this idea even further. This riff à la Deep Purple's "Woman From Tokyo" is made up of an Esus4 and E chord. Your fingers barely move.

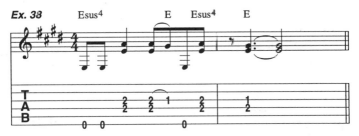

Ex. 39 is a riff based on Led Zeppelin's "Good Times Bad Times."

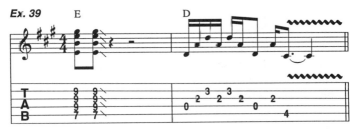

Ex. 40 is a riff in the style of AC/DC's "Back in Black." The chords and the single-note lines act as a call and response.

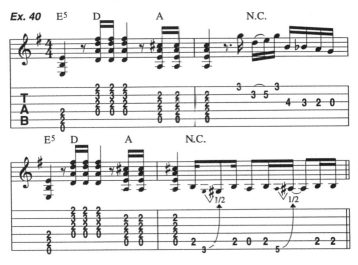

Ex. 41: Another call and response riff can be played with our interpretation of Jimi Hendrix's "Foxey Lady."

Single-note riffs are often used with the power chord, which is made up of the root note of the chord (the A of the A5 chord) and the note which is a perfect 5th away, in this case E. The next set of examples all utilize the power chords along with single-notes.

Ex. 42 is a good example of the power-chord riff. This is our take on Ted Nugent's "Cat Scratch Fever."

Ex. 43 is our interpretation of Neil Young's power-chord riff to "Mr. Soul." Are we the only ones who notice a resemblance to The Stones' "Satisfaction?"

Ex. 44 is a riff based on AC/DC's "Whole Lotta Rosie."

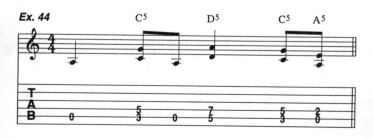

Ex. 45 is a take on Mountain's "Mississippi Queen." Here the power chords introduce the riff and the single-notes finish it.

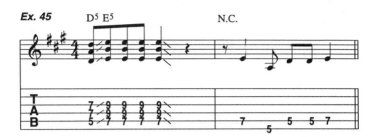

Ex. 46 uses a similar idea to Ex. 45. This is a riff based on Neil Young's "Cinnamon Girl."

Ex. 47 is based on one of the most famous power-chord riffs of all time, Led Zeppelin's "Whole Lotta Love."

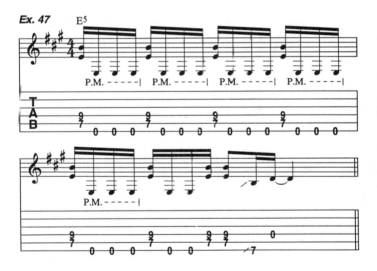

Ex. 48 is à la Metallica's "Seek and Destroy."

Ex. 49 is our take on "Paranoid" from Black Sabbath.
Notice the use of hammer-ons.

Ex. 50 is a simple riff with a lot of impact, based on The
Stones' tune "Shattered."

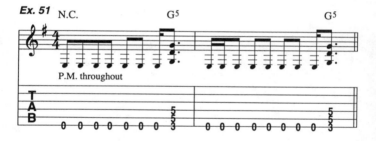

Ex. 51 is also minimal in its note choice, but powerful in its
impact. This is an interpretation of riff to "Electric Head Part
2," by White Zombie.

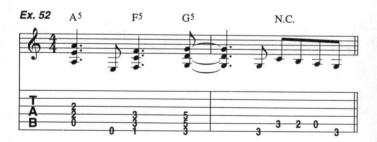

Ex. 52 is our vision of Dio's "Rainbow In The Dark."

Ex. 53 is a take on "Architecture of Aggression" from
Megadeth.

20

The last grouping of riffs in this section move into the more overtly melodic category.

Ex. 54 is à la the Grateful Dead's "Casey Jones."

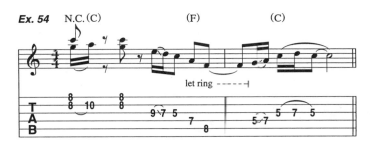

Ex. 55 is our vision of a riff from "Life's Been Good" by Joe Walsh.

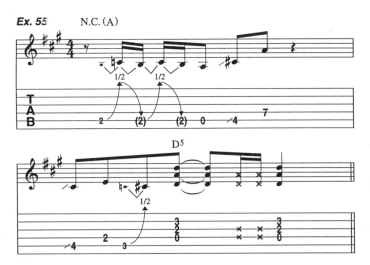

Ex. 56 is a take on "Running from an Angel" by Hootie and The Blowfish.

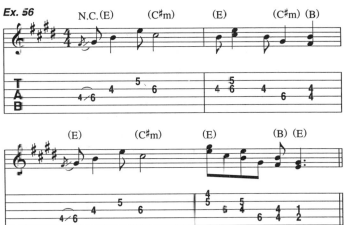

Ex. 57 is an interpretation of "Rotten Apple."

Ex. 58 was inspired by Eric Clapton's riff to "Layla."

Ex. 59 is similar to Neil Young's "Hey Hey My My." Notice how the first four notes come from the A Natural Minor Scale (A,B,C,D,E,F,G) followed by the Am chord.

Ex. 60 is our take on Richie Valens' "La Bamba." The Beatles took this from The Isley Brothers and turned it into one of their first hits, "Twist And Shout."

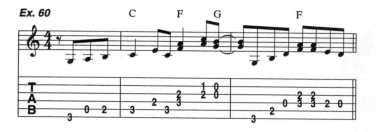

Ex. 61 is à la "Hot for Teacher" by Van Halen. This features legato playing and slides.

Ex. 62 reminds us of the Free song, "Mr. Big." Billy Sheehan
took the title of this song to name his band.

*I can honestly say "Maggie May" changed my life. "Ziggy
Stardust" is another, and so is "Suffragette City." I would say
"Honky Tonk Woman" is one of the best guitar riffs.*
—Gilby Clarke (Guns N' Roses)

POWER-CHORD RIFFS

In this section we are dealing strictly with power chords. The use of power chords often adds muscle and strength to the riff.

Ex.63 clearly underlines the point we just made. Here is a take on Deep Purple's "Smoke on the Water."

Ex. 64 is similar to the power-chord riff that brought the group Yes to the top of the charts with "Owner of a Lonely Heart."

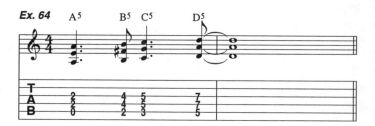

Ex. 65 is at the heart of rock 'n' roll rhythm guitar and an awful lot of blues playing as well. This is something similar to what Eric Clapton played on "I'm Tore Down."

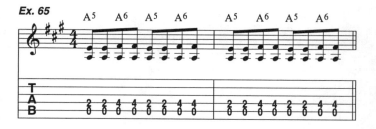

Ex. 66 is from the same vein as the previous example. This time we've interpreted The Eagles' "Already Gone."

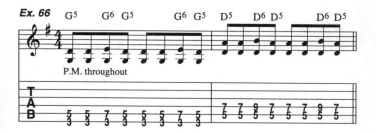

Ex. 67 is our rendition of "More Human Than Human" by White Zombie. This rhythm riff is built on one chord—E5!

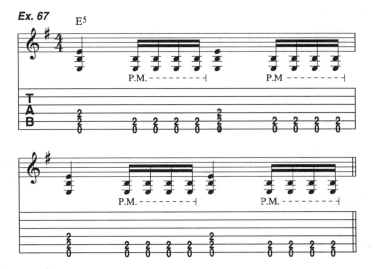

Ex. 68 reminds us of "This Is a Call" from Foo Fighters. The simplicity of this riff does not diminish its impact.

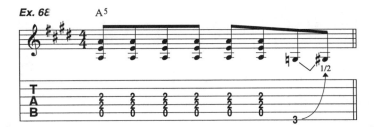

Ex. 69 is similar to "All Day and All of the Night" by The Kinks.

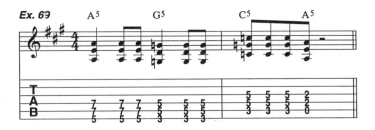

Ex. 70 is an interpretation of "Iron Man" by Black Sabbath.

Ex. 71 is similar to a rhythm riff from "Welcome to the Jungle" by Guns N' Roses.

Ex. 72 reminds us of "Rock You Like A Hurricane" by the Scorpions.

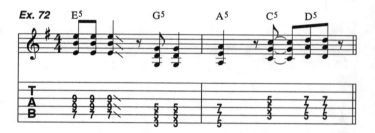

Ex. 73 was inspired by a riff from "Quiet" by Smashing Pumpkins.

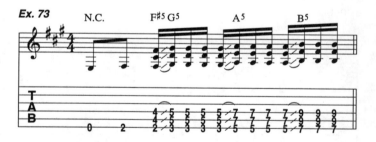

Ex. 74 is our take on how Blue Oyster Cult used rhythm riffs in "Godzilla."

Ex. 75 is similar to what Bush played in their song "Everything Zen."

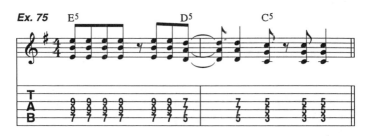

Ex. 76 is à la "Jailbreak" by Thin Lizzy.

Ex. 77 is a take on a rhythm riff from "Sweating Bullets" by Megadeth.

Three riffs that changed your life? Everybody is going to say "Smoke on the Water" and I'm going to say that too. I remember that coming in on the car radio when I was a little kid. I remember that so vividly. It was so powerful. I never remembered the rest of the song. All I remembered was that riff. "Sunshine of Your Love" was powerful in its own way, but it wasn't as powerful as "Smoke on the Water." It was more of a fun thing that you could hum all day. The intro to "Roll Over Beethoven" needs to be first. ELO's version blew me away. Once I first started playing I used to sit in music stores and play that riff over and over. My first showoff song was "Day Tripper." I had it down because I figured if you played it really close to the bridge, it gets that same twang they have.

—Alex Skolnick (Testament)

CHORD-STRUMMING RIFFS

Power chords riffs punch at you. They are meant to snap your head back. Strumming riffs roll into the body. Because the chords are made up of more than just the root and 5th, they push you back with weight as well as power. To understand this, listen to any song by The Who, or, better yet, play the examples below.

Ex. 78 is à la "Substitute" by The Who.

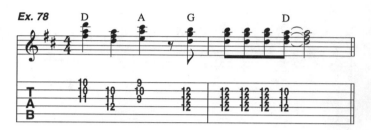

Ex. 79 is another example of how to write a hook with just three chords. This is similar to Jimi Hendrix's rendition of "Wild Thing."

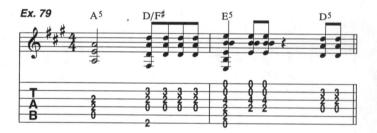

Ex. 80, à la the Clash's "Should I Stay or Should I Go," shows that you can write a memorable riff with just two chords.

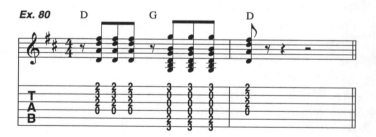

Ex. 81 breaks it down even further. The difference between the two chords in this Santana-like riff from "Oye Como Va" is one note!

Ex. 82 is a classic case of what you can do with one note. Here is a riff where the suspended chord is resolving to a triad, à la The Who's "Pinball Wizard."

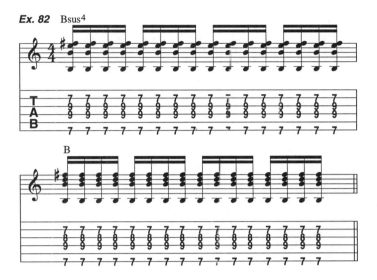

Ex. 83 is another example of suspended chords resolving to triads. This time we interpreted "Nothing Left" by Dokken.

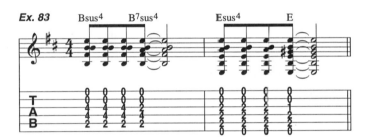

Ex. 84 is a bit of contemporary strumming that reminds us of Def Leppard's "Photograph."

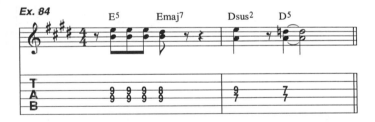

Ex. 85 is our rendition of what Rush has done with two chords in the tune "The Spirit of Radio."

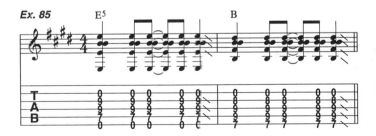

Ex. 86 is another two-chord riff. It's our take on The Doobie Brothers' "Rockin' Down the Highway." Notice the use of rests, which creates a sparse rhythm.

Ex. 87 is a Hendrix-inspired rendition of "Purple Haze."

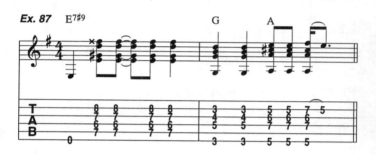

Ex. 88 is built around hammer-ons. It's similar to the James Gang piece, "Funk 49."

Ex. 89 is inspired by Van Halen's "Runnin' with the Devil." It too is a hammer-on based riff.

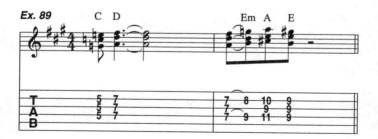

Ex. 90 is a Dire Straits-like run from "Sultans Of Swing."

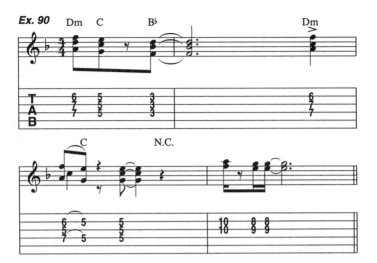

Ex. 91 is similar to what Jimi Hendrix played on "Wait Till Tomorrow."

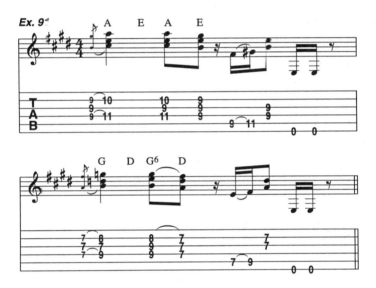

Ex. 92 is a staccato riff arranged from the keyboard of Van Halen's "Jump."

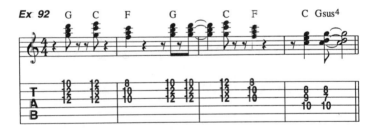

Ex. 93 helped establish alternative music in the '90s, with this Nirvana-like take on "Smells Like Teen Spirit."

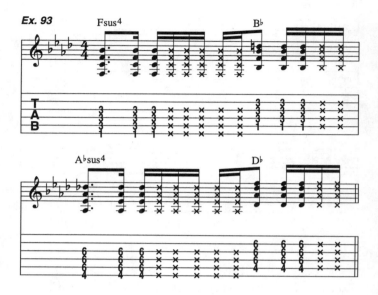

Ex. 94 resembles a Rush riff from "Free Will."

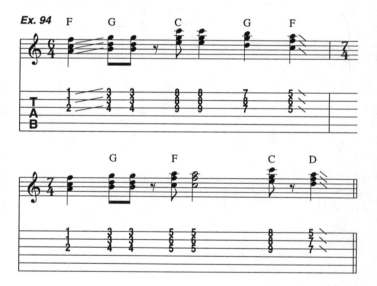

Of the riffs that changed my life, I remember trying to play the line in "YYZ" by Rush. I was into Black Sabbath as a little kid. I remember trying to play "Paranoid." I remember trying to get that Van Halen sound from "Ain't Talkin' About Love." Nobody could ever get that sound.

—*John Petrucci (Dream Theater)*

Arpeggio riffs are played by holding a chord and playing one note after another in sequence, each note sounding separately. This is a time honored idea that has practitioners from The Beatles to The Foo Fighters. Some people play arpeggios with fingers, others with a pick. The choice is yours. For more detail on arpeggios, check out the *Pocket Guide to Acoustic Rock Guitar.*

Ex. 95 is similar to a Rush line from "Tom Sawyer."

Ex. 96 reminds us of "Cinnamon Girl" by Neil Young.

Ex. 97 is à la "Ticket to Ride" by The Beatles.

Ex. 98 is reminiscent of a riff from "This is a Call" by Foo Fighters.

Ex. 99 reminds us of a line from "Black Hole Sun" by Soundgarden.

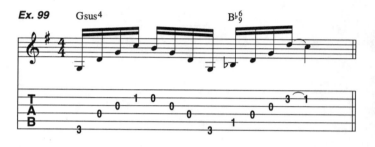

Ex. 100 is similar to "Hey You" by Pink Floyd.

Ex. 101 is à la "Foreclosure of a Dream" by Megadeth.

Ex. 102 reminds us of a line from "Red Barchetta" by Rush.

Ex. 103 was also inspired by Rush. This is our interpretation of 'Entre Nous.'

Ex. 104 sounds similar to "Fall Down" by Toad The Wet Sprocket.

Ex. 105 is à la "Today" from Smashing Pumpkins.

Ex. 106 is like "Every Breath You Take" from The Police.

Ex. 107 is similar to Guns N' Roses "Sweet Child O' Mine."

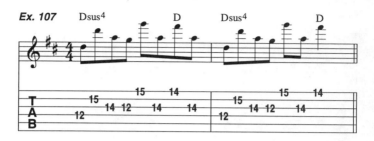

Ex. 108 is our take on The Who's "Behind Blue Eyes."

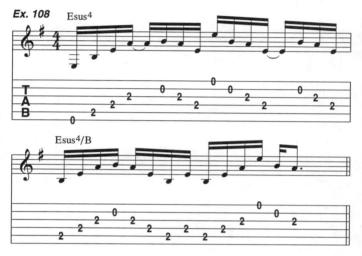

Ex. 109 is à la "Cult of Personality" from Living Colour.

Ex. 110 was inspired by Def Leppard's "Photograph."

Ex. 111 is our take on Def Leppard's "Rock Rock Till You Drop."

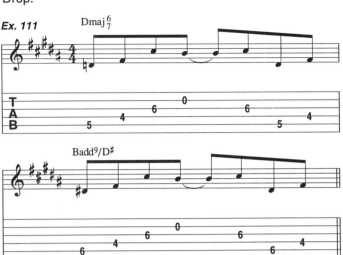

Ex. 112 is a reflection on Dokken's "Nothing Left to Say."

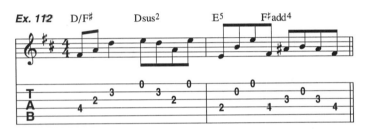

Ex. 113 is similar to "Message in a Bottle" by The Police.

Ex. 114 is our take on Bon Jovi's "Wanted: Dead Or Alive."

Three riffs that changed my life were the organ riff from "Green Onions," Scotty Moore on "Mystery Train," and the solo James Burton took on "Hello Marylou."

—Dave Edmunds

For me it's the power-chord riff to "I've Been Waiting for You" by Neil Young, the opening riff to "Mississippi Queen," by Mountain, and the opening instrumental part in Lou Reed's "Sweet Jane" played by Dick Wagner and Steve Hunter.

—Reeves Gabrels (David Bowie)

"I Was Made to Love Her" by Stevie Wonder with James Jamerson on bass, "Thank You (Faletinme Be Mice Elf Agin)" by Sly and the Family Stone, and "Brave And Strong" by Sly and the Family Stone with Sly on bass.

—Bootsy Collins

I liked the Isley Brothers' "Summer Breeze." That changed me. There is Chuck Berry's ever-popular clichéd intro to "Johnny B. Goode." I wore that out. Then there is B.B. King's "The Thrill is Gone."

—Ernie C (Body Count)

Three riffs that changed my life were "Purple Haze" definitely, "Whole Lotta Love" and a fast song by Al DiMeola called "Race With the Devil on Spanish Highway." My first showoff songs were "Mississippi Queen" and "Aqualung."

—Michael Wilton (Queensrÿche)

Three riffs that changed my life are the opening riff to "Whole Lotta Love," the opening riff to "Taxman," and "Breathe" off of Dark Side of the Moon.

—Chris DeGarmo (Queensrÿche)

You can always pick up a guitar and bash away and think of a good idea.

—Angus Young (AC/DC)*

The following is a list of recordings where many riff-heavy songs reside:

American Beauty – The Grateful Dead

Anthology 2 – The Beatles

Appetite for Destruction – Guns N' Roses

Are You Experienced – The Jimi Hendrix Experience

Back in Black – AC/DC

Bad Motorfinger – Sound Garden

Benefit – Jethro Tull

Boston – Boston

Brothers and Sisters – The Allman Brothers Band

Climbing – Mountain

Cowboys from Hell – Pantera

Crossroads – Eric Clapton

Decade – Neil Young

Diary of a Madman – Ozzy Osbourne

Dirt – Alice in Chains

Hotel California – The Eagles

Kiss Alive II – Kiss

Led Zeppelin II – Led Zeppelin

Machine Head – Deep Purple

Master of Puppets – Metallica

Orleans – Orleans

Paranoid – Black Sabbath

Permanent Waves – Rush

Queen II – Queen

Ten – Pearl Jam

Texas Flood – Stevie Ray Vaughan

The Joshua Tree – U2

The Police Live – The Police

Time is Tight – Booker T and the MGs

Toys in the Attic – Aerosmith

Truth – Jeff Beck Group

Van Halen – Van Halen

Wheels of Fire – Cream

Who's Next – The Who

POCKET GUIDE

Whether you have to get to your lessons or your gig, these great guides fit easily into your guitar case so you never have to be without them!

Ultimate Guitar Chord User's Guide
00697242 . . . . $6.95

Playing Chord Progressions
00696518 . . . . $5.95

Major Pentatonic Scales For Guitar
by John Stix & Yoichi Arakawa
00695013 . . . . $5.95

Minor Pentatonic Scales For Guitar
by John Stix & Yoichi Arakawa
00695014 . . . . $5.95

Acoustic Rock For Guitar
by John Stix & Yoichi Arakawa
00695019 . . . . $5.95

Basic Blues For Rock Guitar
by John Stix & Yoichi Arakawa
00695017 . . . . $5.95

FOR MORE INFORMATION, SEE YOUR LOCAL MUSIC DEALER,
OR WRITE TO:

HAL•LEONARD™ CORPORATION
7777 W. BLUEMOUND RD. P.O. BOX 13819 MILWAUKEE, WI 53213

Prices and availability subject to change without notice.

1295